Quick Travel Guide to

By: Sarah Melland

The Contents

Introduction

Paris (French pronunciation: [paʁi]) is the capital of France and most populous city, with 2,165,423 people living in an area of more than 41 square miles according to the 2019 census, making it the world's 34th most densely populated city. Paris has been referred to be the world's center of banking, diplomacy, business, fashion, gastronomy, science and the arts since the 17th century.

Paris is a major rail, highway, and air transportation hub, with two international airports: Paris–Charles de Gaulle (Europe's second busiest) and Paris–Orly. The Paris Métro, which opened in 1900 and serves 5.23 million passengers daily, is Europe's second-busiest metro system behind the Moscow Metro.

With 262 million passengers in 2015, Gare du Nord is the world's 24th busiest railway station, but the busiest outside of Japan.

The Louvre welcomed 2.8 million visitors in 2021. The Musée d'Orsay, the Musée Marmottan Monet and the Musée de l'Orangerie are known for their Impressionist art collections. The Musée National d'Art Moderne at the Pompidou Centre houses Europe's biggest collection of modern and contemporary art. The paintings of two famous Parisians are on display at the Musée Rodin and the Musée Picasso.

Since 1991, the historical district along the Seine in the city center has been designated as a UNESCO World Heritage Site; notable sites include the Cathedral of Notre Dame de Paris on the Île de la Cité. The Gothic royal chapel of Sainte-Chapelle, also on the Île de la Cité; the Eiffel Tower, built for the Paris Universal Exposition of 1889; the Grand and Petit Palais, built for the Paris Universal Exposition of 1900; the Arc de Triomphe on the Champs-Élysées; and the hill of Montmartre, with its artistic history and its Basilica of Sacré-Coeur.

In 2021, tourism in the Paris region improved, with 22.6 million tourists, a 30% increase over 2020, but still significantly below 2019 levels. Over the course of 2020, the number of visitors from the United States climbed by 237%.

Paris is home to the football club Paris Saint-Germain and the rugby union Stade Français. The 80,000-seat Stade de France is located just north of Paris in the neighboring commune of Saint-Denis, and was erected for the 1998 FIFA World Cup.

On the red clay of Roland Garros, Paris holds the annual French Open Grand Slam tennis event. In 1900 and 1924, the city hosted the Olympic Games. Now, one hundred years later, in 2024, it will host the Summer Olympics again.

The city has hosted the 1938 and 1998 FIFA World Cups, and the 2007 Rugby World Cup. It also hosted the 1960, 1984, and 2016 UEFA European Championships. The Tour de France bicycle race concludes on the Avenue des Champs-Élysées in Paris every July.

Amazing History of Paris, France

A tribe of Celtic Gauls known as the Parisii founded Paris near the end of the third century BC on what is now the Île de la Cité. In 52 BC, Julius Caesar's forces acquired control of the country, ending centuries of conflict between the Gauls and the Romans. In the second century AD, Christianity was introduced, and with the entrance of the Franks in the fifth century, Roman rule came to an end. Clovis I, a Frankish monarch, united Gaul as a kingdom in 508 AD and named Paris after the original Parisii tribe.

During the Middle Ages, Paris flourished. Construction on Notre Dame Cathedral began in the 12th century and lasted almost 200 years. The Marais area, north of the Seine, was drained and settled to create what is now known as the Right Bank.

The legendary Louvre Museum was founded in 1200 as a riverbank stronghold.

The exquisite Sainte Chapelle in 1248, and Sorbonne Université, a prominent French university was founded in 1150 and ceased operations in 1970.

Yes, there were Vikings in Paris' past! In the ninth century, Scandinavian Vikings, also known as Norsemen or Normans, began invading France's western shore. After three centuries of battle, they began to push into Paris. "The Hundred Years War" broke out between Norman England and the Capetian dynasty of Paris, culminating in the French loss at Agincourt in 1415 and English possession of Paris in 1420. In 1429, a 17-year-old girl named Jeanne d'Arc rallied the French army to defeat the English at Orleans. With the exception of the Calais campaign, Louis XIV (the Sun King) succeeded to the throne at the juvenile age of five and kept the monarchy until 1715.

During King Louis XIV's rule, the national treasury was nearly bankrupted as a result of aggressive foreign wars and ever-increasing domestic spending. The palace at Versailles, 23 kilometers (15 miles) south of Paris, is his most visible legacy. Whatever the ups and downs of the French monarchy, they found a way to financially and militarily support the American Revolution. Regardless of this, or maybe because of it, the excesses of Louis XVI (the Sun King's great-great-great-grandson) and his capricious queen, Marie-Antoinette, sparked a revolt in Paris on July 14, 1789. The Bastille prison was besieged by citizens, igniting the French Revolution. In 1453, the English were exiled from France.

At the end of the 1400s, the Renaissance propelled Paris forward, and many of the city's iconic structures and monuments arose during this time. By the late 16th century, Paris was enraged once more, this time over religious issues. In 1572, the St. Bartholomew's Day massacre of 3,000 Huguenots in town to celebrate Henri of Navarre's wedding brought the conflict between the Huguenot Protestants and the Catholics to a new low (King Henri IV).

The History of Paris after the Revolution

The revolution's early populist aspirations swiftly gave way to the Reign of Terror, during which many of the revolution's original "patriots" became uncomfortably familiar with Madame la Guillotine. In 1799, the post-revolutionary administration was strengthened under the leadership of Napoleon Bonaparte, a young Corsican general who assumed the title of First Consul. Napoleon was anointed Emperor of France by the Pope in 1804, and he went on to conquer most of Europe.

Napoleon's desire for conquest led to his downfall, first in Russia in 1812 and then in Belgium at Waterloo in 1815. The contemporary French legal system is based on Napoleon's approach to administration, and many monuments such as the huge Arc de Triomphe were created as a result of his leadership.

Following Napoleon's exile and final defeat at Waterloo, France was ruled by a succession of usually ineffective monarchs until a coup d'etat in 1851 installed Napoleon III, Napoleon's own nephew. Yes, Paris has had two Napoleons! He managed the development of a showy new Paris with broad boulevards, sculptured parks, and – not insignificantly – a modern sewer system during his 17-year reign. For the most part, Napoleon III and his urban planner, Baron Haussmann, gave us the Paris we see today. Almost all of medieval Paris was destroyed, but remnants can still be found in the Marais.

However, like his namesake uncle, young Napoleon's pugnacity resulted in an expensive and ultimately futile war, this time with the Prussians in 1870. When word of their emperor's capture by the enemy reached Paris, people flocked to the streets to demand the establishment of a republic.

Despite its terrible beginnings, the Third Republic ushered in the Belle Epoque's brilliant golden years.

Art Nouveau architecture and a flurry of breakthroughs in the arts and sciences were hallmarks of the Belle Époque. This is when the iconic Eiffel Tower was built (1889). During this time, the Statue of Liberty was sent to America (1886).

By the 1930s, Paris had established itself as a global center for the avant-garde arts and, in some ways, as the world capital for free-thinking intellectuals. The Nazi takeover of Paris in 1940 put an end to this era, and the city remained under German control until August 25, 1944. To give the French the dignity of reclaiming their capital, the Allied forces that retook the city were led by Free French Battalions.

The British and American generals had to negotiate immensely, and Charles De Gaulle's leadership made it possible. After the war, Paris reclaimed its status as a creative hotspot, nurturing a reinvigorated liberalism that culminated in the 1968 student-led "Spring Uprising." The Sorbonne University was occupied, barricades were raised in the Latin Quarter, and nine million people across France were motivated to join a nationwide general strike, drawing attention to their growing discontent with the rigidity of French institutions. (After the allied liberation of France, Charles De Gaulle returns to Paris.)

President Francois Mitterrand launched the futuristic Grands Projets in the 1980s, a series of ambitious construction projects that received considerable support despite the fact that the results were occasionally popular failures.

The more flamboyant examples, such as the Centre Pompidou and the Louvre's glass pyramids, have elicited reactions ranging from outrage to rapture; if nothing else, the projects rekindled debate over the Parisian style and added to the city's illustrious past.

The elegance of Paris has survived to this day because to active preservation efforts, but the city is looking to the future with a massive expansion and upgrading of the metro system (due to be completed by 2030) and a rededication of pedestrian and bike-friendly policies.

A visit to Paris is on any tourist's dream list. Paris remains the city of light and love, and it is a wonderful location to visit.

Fun Facts about Paris

City of Light

You've probably heard people refer to Paris as "The City of Light," but do you know why? There are two ideas about the nickname for Paris. First, it is stated that light in this circumstance denotes intellectuals. It alludes to the city's long history of attracting a large number of writers, artists and scholars. Another explanation is how Paris became known as the "City of Light" because it was one of the first European cities to implement street lighting.

The Louvre is the World's Biggest Art Museum

The Louvre is the world's biggest art collection and museum, housing more than 38,000 works of art, including the most renowned painting of all time, the Mona Lisa. It visited by 10.8 million people in 2018, making it the most visited gallery on the planet!

The Eiffel Tower is not the Most Visited Monument in Paris

The Eiffel Tower, contrary to common opinion, is not the most visited monument in Paris! The Eiffel Tower is considered fourth among Paris' most valuable monuments. Notre-Dame de Paris Cathedral, the Sacré-Coeur Basilica and the Louvre Museum are ranked first, second, and third, respectively. When you're in Paris, make sure to see them all!

Did You Know There is One Dog for Every Seven Parisians?

In Paris, there are more than 300,000 dogs. Dogs are truly man's best friend, but Parisians take it to a new level. In Paris, people care deeply about their pets, spending over half a million dollars to ensure that their dogs receive the greatest care. It's not uncommon to see their owners pampering their pets at a doggy spa.

Second-Busiest Underground Network in Europe

Locals' preferred mode of transportation is the Paris Metro, which is used by approximately five million people per day. It is Europe's busiest subway system, second only to Moscow. Count your stations when using the subway in Paris - you never know where you'll wind up if you don't, as the metro system in most big cities does not announce its stops.

French Came up with the Military "Dress Code"

Paris is the fashion capital, and the majority of the world's most well-known fashion labels are French (Chanel, Louis Vuitton, Dior, Jacquemus, you name it). They were also the ones that came up with the military uniforms. The French were the first to deploy camouflage clothes in the military; the word "camouflage" roughly translates to "make up for the stage."

First "Bloody Mary" was made in Paris

At the Ritz Hotel in Paris, the renowned "Bloody Mary" cocktail was created. This renowned cocktail is said to have been created for the famous novelist Ernest Hemingway. Hemingway requested a drink that didn't have an alcoholic odor. Therefore, he was served vodka blended with tomato juice.

The French army still use carrier pigeons

In Europe, the French army is the only one that still uses carrier pigeons. These pigeons, which are housed near Paris at Mont Valérien, can be used to carry out broadcasts in the event of a severe disaster.

The Paris Syndrome

One of the strangest Parisian facts. This is the most common ailment among Japanese visitors. The Japanese media frequently portrays Paris as the world's most romantic location, with model-like people dressed up on the streets, giving the Japanese a little erroneous impression of the city. As a result, they are frequently disappointed when they arrive since the city fails to meet their inflated expectations.

Parisians declined Tom Cruise's request to become an honorary citizen

The mayor of Paris has passed a resolution prohibiting Tom Cruise from being made an honorary citizen. Tom Cruise is a member of Scientology, a controversial religious organization that has been labeled a cult in France. Tom Cruise wanted to become an honorary citizen of Paris in 2005, but the city's officials refused because of his involvement with Scientology.

Useful French Phrases for Travelers

For Conversation:

1. Bonjour! (Good morning, hello)

2. Bienvenue. (Welcome.)

3. Madame/Monsieur/Mademoiselle (Mrs. /Mr. /Miss)

4. Pardon, excusez-moi. (Pardon, excuse me.)

5. Parlez-vous anglais? (Do you speak English?)

6. Je ne parle pas français. (I do not speak French.)

7. À tout à l'heure! (See you later!)

8. Merci/Merci beaucoup. (Thank you/Thank you very much.)

9. Au revoir! (Goodbye!)

10. De rien. (You're welcome.)

For Information:

11. Pourriez-vous m'aider? (Can you help me?)

12. Pourriez-vous prendre ma photo/notre photo? (Are you able to take my photo/our photo?)

13. Je ne comprends pas. (I do not understand.)

14. Parlez lentement, s'il vous plaît. (Speak slowly, please.)

15. Répétez, s'il vous plait. (Repeat, please.)

16. Où sont des toilettes? (Where are the toilets?)

17. Où est un bon restaurant/un bon café? (Where is a good restaurant/a good café).

18. Où est la plage/le centre-ville? (Where is the beach/city center.)

19. Je cherche le métro/le gare/l'aéroport. (I am searching for the metro/train station/airport.)

20. Je cherche l'hôtel/l'hôpital/la banque. (I am searching for the hotel/hospital/bank.)

For Direction:

21. Où sommes-nous? (Where are we?)

22. C'est à gauche. (It's to the left.)

23. C'est à droite. (It's to the right.)

24. C'est tout droit. (It's straight ahead.)

25. Est-ce que c'est loin/proche? (Is it far/close?)

For Transportation:

26. Où est le guichet? (Where is the ticket window?)

27. Je voudrais regarder l'horaire. (I would like to look at the schedule.)

28. Je voudrais réserver un billet. (I would like to reserve a ticket.)

29. Je voudrais acheter un billet aller simple/aller-retour pour Paris. (I would like to purchase a one-way ticket/a round-trip ticket.)

30. À quelle heure faut-il arriver? (What time should it arrive?)

For Accommodations:

31. Quelles chambres avez-vous de disponible? (What rooms do you have available?)

32. Est-ce qu'il y a de climatisation? (Is there air conditioning?)

33. Je voudrais une chambre pour deux. (I would like a double room.)

34. Je voudrais annuler ma réservation. (I would like to cancel my reservation.)

35. À quelle heure est-ce qu'il faut régler la note? (At what time should we check out?)

For Shopping:

36. Où sont les magasins? (Where are the shops?)

37. Où est le centre-commercial? (Where is the mall?)

38. Est-ce que je peux payer avec une carte de crédit? (Can I pay with a credit card?)

39. À quelle heure est-ce que s'est ouvert? (At what time is it open?)

40. À quelle heure est-ce que s'est fermé? (At what time is it closed?)

41. Je cherche un sac/une carte postale/un livre. (I am searching for a bag/a postcard/a book.)

42. Combien ça coûte? (How much does it cost?)

43. C'est trop cher! (It's too expensive!)

44. C'est bon marché! (It's a great deal!)

45. C'est bon/mal/terrible. (It's good/bad/terrible.)

For Dining:

46. La carte/le menu, s'il vous plaît. (The menu/fixed-price menu, please.)

47. Je voudrais un café. (I would like a coffee.)

48. Je voudrais un verre. (I would like a glass.) *Usually, a glass of beer

49. Je voudrais de l'eau. (I would like some water.)

50. L'addition, s'il vous plaît. (The bill, please.)

French Etiquette and Manners

Before visiting France, it is critical to understand French etiquette. In most places, the French have rigorous norms of behavior, so learning some fundamental French etiquette will save you a lot of time and humiliation. There are some formal standards to know, especially in areas like the metro, stores, and restaurants, to ensure that you respect the French and their culture. All of these recommendations, from tipping to greeting people in stores, can help you have a better time in France!

When you walk into a store or a restaurant, say "Bonjour."

When you come into a store, restaurant or bar, it is critical you greet the people who work there. "Bonjour" (or "Bonsoir" in the evening) is a courteous greeting which also serves as an introduction to your

encounter with the waiter or shop assistant. If you don't say anything, the attendants are unlikely to greet you, seat you, or serve you. In restaurants, this is especially true. Even if you don't understand French, a simple "bonjour" will go a long way! Also, upon leaving, remember to say "Au revoir!"

Talking Loudly

The French, especially after certain hours and on the metro, are a quiet people. So, to avoid getting chastised for being excessively loud, try to keep the volume low in most settings. Even in cities like Paris, you'll notice how quiet the metros and buses are, and being loud on them is considered as a nuisance by people who are simply trying to get to work or home in peace. If you're staying somewhere, make sure you don't speak too loudly or have any loud music playing after 10 p.m., because you'll either get into an argument with an enraged neighbor or they'll call the cops. In France, it's preferable to keep everything at a lower volume.

Tipping in France

In France, do you tip? This is likely the most frequently asked question by visitors, and it can be perplexing. Waiters in France are paid a minimum wage, and all bills contain a service charge. As a result, tipping is not required. It is, nevertheless, a manner of expressing your gratitude for excellent service. You can give as little or as much as you like because there is no predefined amount. A good gratuity is usually between 10% and 20% of the total bill. It's worth noting that tips are not included in your credit card payment, so you'll have to pay cash.

Metro and Bus Etiquette

On the bus or metro, you'll see placards requesting passengers to give up their seats to the old, crippled, or pregnant. Although this may appear to be a no-brainer, many tourists overlook it. Especially while trying to find out how to use the public transportation system and where they are supposed to go. It's also worth noting that you must stand if you're seated on the seats near the metro's doors when it's full. This is to allow more individuals to enter.

Drinking in Public

It is permitted to drink in most public locations in Paris. So, whether you're having a picnic at the Tuileries, the Luxembourg Gardens, or along the Seine, you can pair your nibbles with a delicious bottle of wine. However, drinking on public transportation is prohibited, and being inebriated in public is a crime.

Don't Take "Non!" for an Answer

The French are known for being open, honest, and always up for a challenge. 'Non!' is frequently the initial reaction to a request. 'But don't surrender!' Try to look at this type of odd behavior as a challenge. 'Non! If you're assigned a table near the door at a restaurant and you'd prefer to sit somewhere warmer, make some cheery but theatrical gestures to imply you're freezing, and your wish may be fulfilled. Accept the oddity and have fun with it.

If someone cuts you off in line, don't freak out.

If you find yourself in a train station, airport, market, or anywhere else where you might expect people to form a line, you'll quickly discover that in France, waiting your turn is not the norm. The French would take gold in line-jumping if it became an Olympic sport. If their grandma wasn't already pushing past them on the bus, people would push past her to be first. Surprisingly, once everyone is on board, people become more courteous and begin providing seats to others who require them.

Don't Expect Speedy Service

Take note, impatient New Yorkers: salespeople will not approach you in a store like they would in the United States. This may appear to be poor customer service, but they are simply providing you with space to browse. We think that anything worth doing should be done well and wisely, therefore taking your time is an important component of French culture. In a restaurant, the waitress will allow you plenty of time to peruse the menu. You won't be shooed out of a French restaurant as soon as you complete your coffee. You can relax and enjoy yourself once you've finished your meal.

This guideline may be broken in Paris, which is more fast-paced and where everyone has somewhere they need to be ten minutes ago. Outside of Paris, though, the pace slows considerably. The further south you travel, the less punctual people become and the less they will like being rushed.

A Formal, Polite Greeting Goes a Long Way

Speak French if you're in France. Even if it's just a few basic sentences, make an attempt at the start of a conversation. Many French individuals will gladly put you out of your pain and immediately switch to English. Always greet individuals with a polite "Bonjour Madame/Monsieur" (or "Bonsoir" in the evening) and err on the formal side. Servers, sales assistants, tour guides, and hotel workers are all included. You'll almost certainly receive better service.

Just Don't Quote "Lady Marmalade"

The 'Voulez-vous...?' phrase should not be used in French, ' from the song "Lady Marmalade." It's not that French people aren't amusing, it's simply the joke hasn't been humorous in France for a long time.

Slow down if you're speaking English.

Consider what would happen if someone approached you in your hometown and began speaking quickly in French. You'd be perplexed and even terrified, depending on where you live. Put yourself in the shoes of a French person. Their English may appear to be superior to your French, but they may not understand your accent or mannerisms. The majority of French people learn British English in school and are unfamiliar with common American idioms. What is the most effective strategy? Slowly and clearly express yourself. Alternatively, if you want to utilize this chance to perfect your British impersonation, go for it.

Don't Attempt Small Talk with a French Person

A comfortable silence is far better to pointless chit-chat in France. Small-talking foreigners may find this awkward. It's not that they're unfriendly, they're just reserved and formal among strangers. Don't ask someone you've just met about their personal life, such as their jobs, families or even what they did last weekend. You're merely having polite conversation, but if you go too personal too quickly, French people will become irritated. Keep it relevant by focusing on current events, sports, the arts and gastronomy.

Don't Mess with the Menu—and Don't Ask for a Box

In the United States, it's common to request no onions and cheddar instead of mozzarella. Unless you have an allergy, this is a massive no-no in France. If you ask for a bag or box to put your leftovers in, expect some raised eyebrows. Most restaurants in France prioritize quality over quantity, therefore the portions (which are far smaller than in the United States) are considered adequate. If you see waiters offering boxes to other customers, ask for one.

Don't Ask for a Coffee to Go Either

It's not cool to ask for a coffee to go unless you're in a Starbucks. It's important to remember that doing things the "French way" entails taking your time. You're not rushing because you're on vacation. Take a seat on the terrace and enjoy your coffee while people-watching.

Don't Bring Bottle of Wine to a House Party

Arrive up to fifteen minutes late and don't bring a bottle of wine if you've been invited to dinner — it's like saying your host's wine isn't good enough. Always wait until the host says "Bon appétit!" before eating. Finally, once you've had your fill of wine, leave your glass full or they'll keep refilling it. The sight of an empty wine glass infuriates the French.

Never Leave a Bathroom Door Open in France

The French keep the majority of their doors closed in their homes. Closed doors demarcate the border between a person's private and social lives, thus it's advisable to stay in rooms with open doors unless you know the individual well. The restroom is the one exception. It is a locked door you can open, but you should never leave it even slightly open when you leave. In France, always close the bathroom door behind yourself.

The French Love to Argue. Don't Take It Personally

In French society, raucous after-dinner disputes are profoundly ingrained. When René Descartes, a 17th-century philosopher, said you have to look at both sides of an argument to get to the truth of a topic, the French took it to heart. They'll even dispute over points they don't agree with to keep things interesting. Foreigners may find their perseverance and dramatic gestures irritating or even violent, but they don't mean it that way — they're just having fun.

About French Kissing…

In France, it is customary to 'faire la bise,' or kiss somebody while greeting, thanking or saying goodbye. For foreigners, this French custom presents a slew of questions: are your lips supposed to brush their cheek or not? How many kisses do you give each other? What do you do with your hands, anyway? You could end up kissing a bunch of people you've never met before at a party and not even know their names by the end. The best course of action is to follow the French person's lead. Most individuals kiss once on each cheek, with the lips touching the flesh or not. As long as you remember your Bonjour Madame's and Merci Beaucoup's, you'll be off to a great start.

Other Weird Things that are Prohibited in France:

- Swimming in Fountains
- Feeding Pigeons (which can result in a fine up to 450€).
- Crossing the Street when the sign is red (4€ fine).
- Drinking at work, except it if its wine, beer or cider.
- Calling your pet pig Napoleon.

Top Attractions

You've probably heard a lot of things about Paris. It's possible you've been there before. However, Paris is a city with so many places to see – from world-class museums to lesser-known hidden jewels – that the adventures it provides can never be exhausted.

Eiffel Tower

The Eiffel Tower, Paris' most famous landmark, was built for the 1889 World Exposition and stands a staggering height of almost 300 meters. A trip up the tower's elevator will take you to the top, where you can take in the view and see the engineer Gustave Eiffel's secret residence on exhibit.

Open daily from 9 a.m. to 11 p.m., except on July 14, where it is closed for their huge fireworks display.

Notre-Dame Cathedral

The Notre-Dame Cathedral (Notre-Dame de Paris) was erected in 1163 and features awe-inspiring architectural characteristics such as rose windows, beautiful sculptures, and Gothic woodwork. It also serves as the backdrop for Victor Hugo's classic novel *The Hunchback of Notre-Dame.*

Arc de Triomphe – Champs-Élysées

The Arc de Triomphe (Triumphal Arch) is the most famous and emblematic triumphal arch in the world, standing at the western end of the bustling Champs-Élysées. Some of France's historic wins, wars, and notable military leaders are engraved on the surfaces. It is one of the most famous sights in Paris.

From 10 a.m. to 9:45 p.m., except on the January 1, May 1, May 8, July 14, November 11, and December 25.

Montmartre – Wall of Love

Montmartre is a large hill northeast of Paris best known for its artistic setting, where during the Belle Époque a number of world-renowned artists, including Monet, Picasso and Renoir, were stationed. Take a pause at the Wall of Love (Le Mur des Je t'aimes) in Montmartre, where the phrase "I love you" is written 311 times in 250 languages.

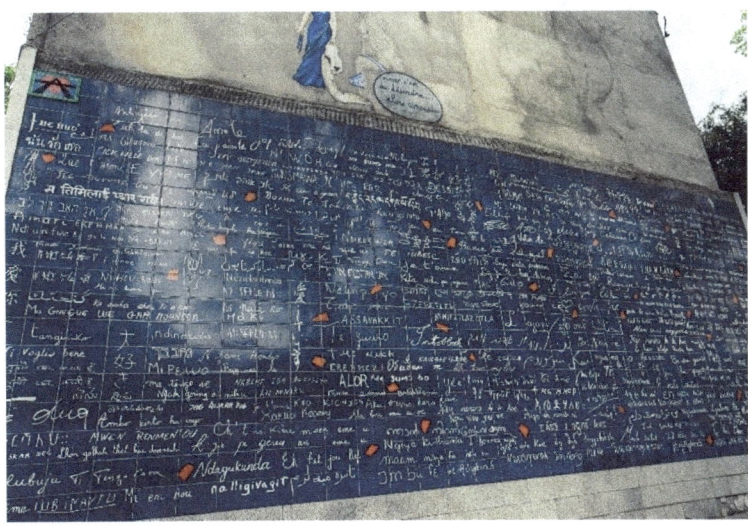

Sacré-Coeur Basilica

The Basilica du Sacré-Coeur is a Roman Catholic church on the Montmartre slope. It is a well-known Parisian landmark and a regular stop on Montmartre tours. Want a workout? Walk the stairs to the top to see the best views of the city.

From 6 a.m. until 10:30 p.m., every day.

Moulin Rouge

Close to Montmartre, the legendary cabaret Moulin Rouge – the spiritual birthplace of modern can-can dance – offers dazzling nighttime shows, the most famous of which are Crazy Horse, Moulin Rouge, and Lido de Paris.

A dinner and show, a show, a VIP evening, or a "matinée" can all be booked.

Tuileries Garden

Take a break in the Tuileries Garden, which is just close to the Louvre, and soak up the afternoon sun while admiring the French formal garden architecture. It's worth noting that there's a little amusement park nearby, which would be ideal if you're traveling with kids.

Open daily from 7:30 a.m. to 7:30 p.m. from September to March, and from 7 a.m. to 9 p.m. the rest of the year.

Panthéon – Latin Quarter

The Panthéon located in the dynamic Latin Quarter houses a crypt containing the tombs of well-known French figures such as Voltaire, Victor Hugo and Marie Curie. A visit to the Panthéon will also bring you to its surrounding Latin Quarter – a lively student neighborhood known for quaint bookstores as well as cheerful cafés and bistros.

Place de la Bastille – Bastille Market

The Place de la Bastille (Bastille Square) is the former locale of the Bastille prison where the "Storming of the Bastille" took place and marked the start of the French Revolution. It is nice to also have a tour of the Bastille Market nearby where a huge range of products are offered.

Versailles Palace

The Versailles Palace, which is frequently ranked as one of the best locations to see in Paris, emanates the lavish grandeur of French Baroque architecture. The opulent mansion and its sprawling gardens will easily occupy one or perhaps two days if  you tour them all. The most popular attraction near Paris is the Versailles Palace.

Catacombs of Paris

The Catacombs of Paris are a massive underground collection of bones and ossuaries. These subterranean ossuaries sprang from overcrowded graves in 18th-century Paris, and more than six million bodies were relocated to one massive cemetery. Imagine a network of  caves and tunnels beneath your feet, all lined with skulls and bones!

Open daily from 10 a.m. to 7.30 p.m., except Mondays, January 1, and May 1.

Parc des Garnier

The Palais Garnier Opera House (also known as Opéra Garnier) is a landmark of the Opéra area that has an elegant theatre and is the home of the famed Paris Opera Ballet. Include a ballet performance on your bucket list, and you will not be disappointed.

Galeries Lafayette

The glittering Galeries Lafayette offers the finest shopping experience in Paris. The department store, which is located in the upscale Opéra area, spans three blocks and houses some of the most prestigious brands, including Chanel, Hermès, and Louis Vuitton. Don't forget to visit the building's top floor for a spectacular view of Paris.

Open every day, from 9:30 a.m. to 8:30 p.m. Monday-Saturday, from 11 a.m. to 8 p.m. on Sunday.

Sainte Chapelle

The Sainte Chapelle is a Gothic royal chapel with one of the most stunning stained-glass interiors in the world. Its collection of stained glass from the thirteenth century is regarded as one of the most extensive in the world.

Open every day from 9 a.m. to 5 p.m., except on January 1, May 1, December 25.

Pont Alexandre III

The Pont Alexandre III, which connects the Champs-Élysées and Eiffel Tower neighborhoods, is the most beautiful and luxurious bridge that spans the Seine. The Pont Alexandre III, which was built for the 1900 World Exposition and is now a designated Historical Monument, is considered one of the most beautiful river crossings in the world.

Tour Montparnasse

The Tour Montparnasse (Montparnasse Tower) is the city of Paris's lone skyscraper. Despite its eccentric appearance, a visit to the rooftop will provide you with an unrestricted 360° panoramic view of the entire city, which is extremely beautiful.

Open every day, from 9:30 a.m. to 11 p.m.

Disneyland Paris

Visit Disneyland Paris, where you may meet your favorite Disney characters in its two theme parks – Disneyland Paris and Walt Disney Studios Park – and marvel at the magical surroundings!

Open every day, from 10 a.m. to 11 p.m.

Le Bon Marché Rive Gauche

The Pont Neuf is the oldest surviving bridge over the Seine. The old stone bridge, built during medieval times, consists of two distinct spans connecting the Île de la Cité – the island in the center of the river – to the left and right banks.

Le Crazy Horse

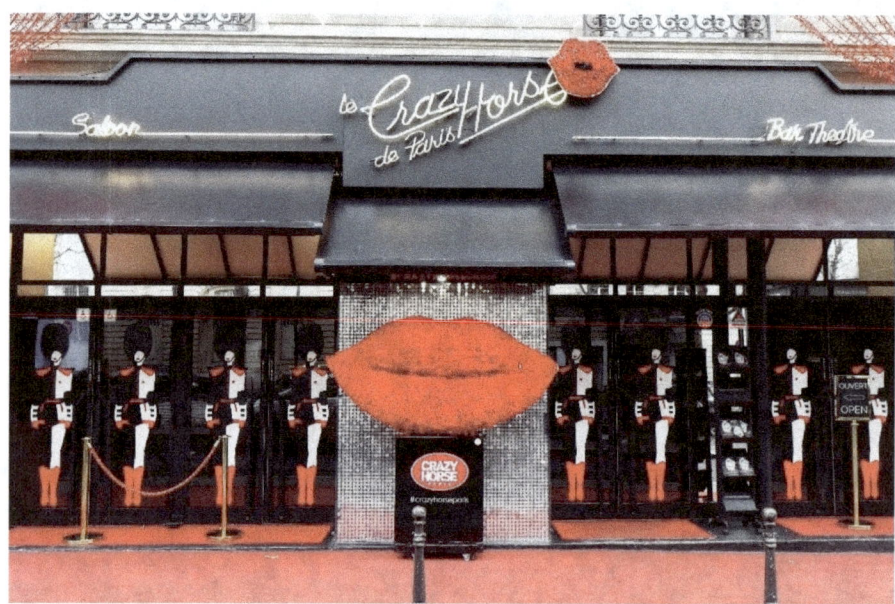

The art du nu (it's a nudie revue!) of Le Crazy Horse, one of the more risqué players on the Parisian cabaret scene, initially opened its doors in 1951 under the direction of the great Alain Bernardin. It still attracts a large number of visitors. It is still oriented to all things feminine and sexual, but only within specific parameters: doppelganger dancers with odd stage names like Enny Gmatic and Hippy Bang Bang all have the same physical measurements. (Girls are legally obligated to have the same height nipples and hips.) Expect a lot of rainbow-colored light and strategically placed black tape. A respectable, old-school cabaret.

Les Passages Couverts

In the eighteenth and nineteenth centuries, glass-roofed shopping galleries abound in the neighborhoods surrounding the Grands Boulevards, serving as elegant forerunners to today's shopping malls. These hidden corridors allowed you to cut corners, avoid the elements, or (ooh la la!) sneak a forbidden kiss with your partner in relative secrecy. Unfortunately, the service is no longer available, but nowadays, passageways couverts are ideal for an afternoon of retail therapy.

Street Art in Paris

Since the 1960s, Paris has had a thriving street art movement, which has only expanded in size since then. In the city's suburbs, outer arrondissements, and center, there is enough of wall space for local and foreign artists to get creative with their spray cans and turn entire areas into outdoor art galleries.

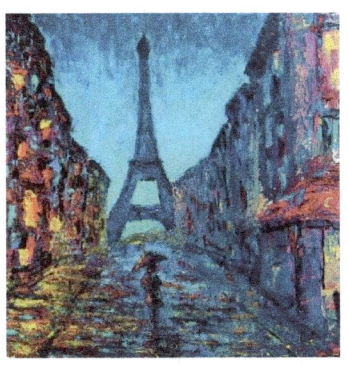

La Coulee Verte

The abandoned train rails connecting Bastille and Vincennes have been reclaimed as La Coulée Verte, a lush, attractive five-kilometer footpath with elevated gardens, the Jardin de Reuilly, and tree-lined cycle paths. Start near the Bastille and make your way to one of the Avenue Daumesnil stairwells for panoramic views of the city. It's so beautiful that it might easily take an entire day to see it all. Pack a picnic and stop in the Jardin de Reuilly, where Paris's first sparkling water fountain may be found (there are now around ten more). Then there's the magnificent Bois de Vincennes, which features lakes and lush, shaded parkland.

Canal Saint-Martin

During Napoleon's reign, the Canal Saint-Martin was constructed between 1805 and 1825. It was built to deliver drinking water and commodities to the Imperial capital, but it has since been home to companies and industrial warehouses since the late 1800s.

Many of those factories have since been converted into lofts for Paris's ever-growing bobo (Bohemian-Bourgeois) community, and the quayside is lined with hundreds of bars, restaurants, and stores. Its sturdy iron footbridges and picturesque locks are popular sites for weekend picnics and treks, especially on Sundays and holidays when cars are prohibited and the roads are only open to hikers and bicycles.

Museums

The Louvre

The world's most visited museum, has a sleek glass pyramid at its entrance. Once inside, you'll be astounded by the extensive art collection, which includes some of the most famous works of art, like Leonardo da Vinci's "Mona Lisa," Michelangelo's "Dying Slave," the "Winged Victory of Samothras," and "Venus de Milo.

Open from 9 a.m. to 6 p.m. every day except Tuesday.

Musée d'Orsay

The Musée d'Orsay (Orsay Museum) is one of Europe's largest museums, focusing on French art from 1848 to 1914. It houses the world's largest collection of impressionist and post-impressionist masterpieces, including Monet, Renoir, Cézanne, and Van Gogh's works. The building's uniqueness stems from its backstory. It was once the Orsay station before being transformed into a museum by Valéry Giscard d'Estaing (French President, 1974-1981).

Open every day, except on Monday, May 1 and December 25, from 9:30 a.m. to 6 p.m.

Musée de l'Orangerie

The Musée de l'Orangerie is an art gallery of impressionist and post-impressionist paintings located in the west corner of the Tuileries Garden next to the Place de la Concorde in Paris.

Musée National Picasso-Paris

The Musée Picasso is an art gallery located in the Hôtel Salé in rue de Thorigny, in the Marais district of Paris, France, dedicated to the work of the Spanish artist Pablo Picasso.

Musée Rodin

The Musée Rodin in Paris, France, is a museum that was opened in 1919, primarily dedicated to the works of the French sculptor Auguste Rodin. It has two sites: the Hôtel Biron and surrounding grounds in central Paris, as well as just outside Paris at  Rodin's old home, the Villa des Brillants at Meudon, Hauts-de-Seine.

Musée Marmottan Monet

Musée Marmottan Monet is an art museum in Paris, France, dedicated to artist Claude Monet. The collection features over three hundred Impressionist and Post-Impressionist paintings by Claude Monet, including his 1872 Impression, Sunrise.

Musée National d'Art Moderne

The Musée National d'Art Moderne is the national museum for modern art of France. It is located in Paris and is housed in the Centre Pompidou in the 4th arrondissement of the city. In 2021 it ranked 10th in the List of most visited art museums in the world, with 1,501,040 visitors. It is one of the largest museums for modern and contemporary art.

Quirky Places to Visit

A Weird Taxidermy Museum

If you're in the Saint-Germain-des-Prés area, don't miss the Maison Deyrolle. This taxidermy and entomology shop/museum specializes in taxidermy and entomology (the study and categorization of articulated animals, particularly insects), and you'll find a type of curiosity cabinet filled with insects, shells, stuffed animals, and other natural wonders. This area is designed to dazzle your eyes, whether you are a collector, a natural science lover, or just a curious visitor.

Eat at a Restaurant in The Dark

This restaurant will shake your connection to food up. The concept of Dans le Noir ("in the darkness") is to serve customers in pitch-black, therefore, you cannot see what is on your plate, but you will love it anyway. Only blind or visually-impaired people serve in here.

Studio 28

You want to see a movie to change things up? Visit Studio 28 for a fantastic experience in a relaxing and creative setting. This theatre offers regular previews that will appeal to movie buffs looking for a relaxing experience in a suitable architectural setting. Before or after the screening, a winter garden will welcome you for a cup of tea or coffee as you eat homemade cookies.

A Very Cool Artistic Squat in Paris

59 Rivoli (in French only) is an artistic community that was created at 59 rue de Rivoli. Ten artists settled in this building to live and have their studio there after it was abandoned by a national bank and by public authorities. Today this seven-floor "squat" is absolutely legal and welcomes visitors for free. About thirty artists present their studios and their works; as for the gallery, it offers several exhibitions. In here, every genre rubs shoulders with one another: street art, painting, sculpture, and even music!

A Digital Immersion into Art

The Ateliers des Lumières, the first digital art center in Paris, is housed in a former smelting plant in the 11th district. This center's ten-meter-high walls, 140 projectors, and 50 speakers on 2,000 m2 allow you to be immersed in master paintings, such as Gustav Klimt's. A unique experience not to be missed!

Finding Quirky Architecture in Paris

Have you recently visited the Eiffel Tower or the Champs de Mars? You may not realize it, but you are within walking distance of an architectural oddity worth seeing: the Lavirotte Building. It is an odd and whimsical structure that stands opposite the Eiffel Tower. It is designed in a distinctive, unusual, and unexpected style.

Its embellishments are revolutionary, exaggerated, and suggestive of a variety of historical periods.

A Very Colorful Basketball Field

The nicest basketball field is in Pigalle in the 9th district: the Pigalle Playground. As it is located between two buildings, this field does not have the regulatory measurements, and the rubber floor absorbs the ball's noises in order to avoid disturbances for the

neighbors. The very flashy colors – purple, yellow, and pink – make it a nice place to play basketball. The field is loved by photographers and it is undoubtedly one of Paris Instagrammers' favorite places!

Best Restaurants

L'Astrance

L'Astrance, a three-Michelin-star restaurant, ranks among the greatest in the world, provides the ultimate fine dining experience in Paris.

Chef Pascal Barbot, who studied at Arpège under Alain Passard, is known for his simple but fantastic meals with unexpected flavors. Instead of relying on salt, pepper, cream, or butter—all of which Barbot adamantly avoids—exotic ingredients like miso and Chinese dates are used to enhance the flavor.

Jòia

Hélène Darroze, the world's greatest female chef, has opened her second restaurant, Jòia.

The menu is centered on comfort food from Darroze's hometown, just outside of the French Basque Country, with a dash of global flavors thrown in for good measure. The Landes region's roasted chicken, as well as the fusion of crêpes mille-feuille and matcha, are must-tries.

You're in luck: one of Paris' most distinctive wine lists is right here to quench your thirst. All of the vintage wines are made by vigneronnes, or female winemakers.

David Toutain

David Toutain creates some of Paris' most innovative and daring cuisine. Toutain, a Normandy native who formerly worked at Arpège alongside Alain Passard, was given his second Michelin star in January 2019. The restaurant's daily-changing menu is chock-full of creative and visually appealing meals. Think grilled eel with black sesame sauce or Toutain's famous egg yolk with cumin caramel creme for flavors that are as surprising as they are delectable.

Aux Bons Crus

From the red-and-white checkered tablecloths to the plastic bread baskets, Aux Bons Crus, a traditional Paris bistro full of old-world charm, has a classic roadside diner décor.

Simple yet distinctive dishes with homey flavors, such as entrecôte steak or pot-au-feu, are on the menu. The wine list in the cellar is broad, making it simple to pick the ideal complement for your meal.

La Bourse et la Vie

The old-fashioned bistro La Bourse et la Vie is a hidden gem. It's led by Daniel Rose, a French-trained American chef who rose to prominence with his French restaurant, Le Coucou, in Manhattan.

Rose is a classic French cook who enjoys bringing old dishes back to life. Comforting classics like veal pot-au-feu and roasted chicken are among his specialties. The star of the menu, however, is his legendary steak-frites, which are unrivaled in the city.

Clamato

Clamato seafood bar is currently one of Paris' hottest restaurants. It is located next door to Théo Pourriat and Michelin-starred chef Bertrand Grébaut's famed restaurant Septime. Tuna tartare, smoked shrimp, octopus carpaccio, and other dishes on the daily-changing menu are outstanding examples of their innovation. Clamato also has a great selection of natural wines that have been carefully chosen.

Breizh Café

Breizh Café, owned by Brittany-born chef Bertrand Larcher, is, as any Parisian will tell you, the best crêperie in the city.

Farmers' market eggs, Bordier butter, and stone-milled organic flour are just a few of the high-quality components used by Larcher. Traditional savory galettes with ham, cheese, and egg are available, or get creative with toppings like smoked duck breast.

Crêpes for dessert are available in both traditional and Asian fusion tastes (Lacher's wife is Japanese). Not only that, but the café also has a large selection of artisanal ciders from Brittany that you should try.

Hugo & Co

Chef Tomy Gousset, a Cambodian-born chef, opened Hugo & Co, a sophisticated Parisian bistro with a New York flair, following the enormous success of his first restaurant. Needless to say, it was a huge success right away.

Hugo & Co was named 2019's bistro of the year, and for good reason: the cuisine is out of this world. It's full of delights like steamed artichokes with curried hummus and smoked mackerel with shiitake mushrooms, which are inspired by international street food.

Worst Restaurants in Paris

Thousands of internet voters have spoken out, naming and shaming the worst eateries and clubs in the city. The black list even includes some well-known Anglos-friendly restaurants. Determine whether you've been eating in the incorrect locations.

Here is the complete worst of Paris restaurants and clubs list based on the thelocalfr blog:

Worst service

1. Le Pierrot, 67 avenue de la Motte-Picquet, 75015

2. Les Etages, 5 rue de Buci, 75006

3. La Gueuze, 19 rue Soufflot, 75005

4. Le Tournesol, 9 rue de la Gaité, 75014

5. L'Atelier, 95 Boulevard du Montparnasse, 75006

Biggest rip-off

1. Le Georges, 19 Rue Beaubourg, 75004

2. Le Départ Saint Michel, 1 Place Saint-Michel, 75005

3. Le Bastille, 8 Place de la Bastille, 75011

4. L'American Dream, 21 Rue Daunou, 75002

5. L'Ice Kube Bar, 5 Passage Ruelle, 75018

Worst disappointment

1. Le Wanderlust, 32 Quai d'Austerlitz, 75013

2. Le Silencio, 142 Rue Montmartre, 75002

3. Les Ombres, 7 Quai Branly, 75007

4. La Perle, 78 Rue Vieille du Temple, 75003 Paris

5. Le bar à Huîtres – Montparnasse, 112 Boulevard du Montparnasse, 75014

Worst bathroom

1. Le Black Dog, 26 Rue des Lombards, 75004

2. Le Point éphémère, 200 Quai de Valmy, 75010

3. Le Merle Moqueur, 11 Rue de la Butte aux Cailles, 75013

4. Le KFC de Châtelet, 35 Boulevard de Sébastopol, 75001

5. Le Syphax, 26 Rue de Châteaudun, 75009

Worst decor

1. Le President, 124 Rue du Faubourg du Temple, 75011

2. Flam's, 32 Avenue du Maine, 75015

3. La Pachanga, 8 Rue Vandamme, 75014

4. La Casa Pepe, 5 Rue Mouffetard, 75005

5. Le Palais du Kashmir, 77 Rue du Poteau, 75018

Hotels for Everyone

Best Luxury Hotels in Paris

Hotel De Crillon, a Rosewood Hotel, Paris

Hôtel de Crillon, which dates back to 1758, has an unmatched view of Place de la Concorde. After a four-year restoration, the building reopened in 2018. With its history serving as a fascinating backdrop for its modern-day story. Master craftsmen, artists and designers worked diligently during the hotel's shutdown to establish a careful yet delicate balance between conservation and transformation. Karl Lagerfeld, the late fashion designer, designed two extraordinary suites called "Les Grands Appartements," which reflect his personal and aesthetic sense of French flair and modernism. The Hôtel de Crillon also has good dining options, a gorgeous pool area, and a small spa.

Shangri-la Hotel, Paris

The Shangri-La Paris, built in 1896, as the mansion of Prince Roland Bonaparte (Napoleon's grandson), is a symbol of style and elegance. The hotel was restored by famous architect Richard Martinet and interior designer Pierre-Yves Rochon to give a distinctly Parisian experience, combining a feeling of history and grandeur with contemporary comfort and service. The hotel's breathtaking views of the Eiffel Tower underline its standing as one of Paris' finest hotels, while its central location in the 16th arrondissement guarantees easy access to the city's most famous attractions. The hotel's pool is one of the largest in Paris. Remember to take a culinary journey to Shang Palace, France's only Michelin-starred Chinese restaurant.

The Ritz Paris

The legendary Paris grande dame, where Princess Diana spent her final night, reopened in 2016 after a four-year makeover by renowned architect Thierry W. Despont restored the house to its previous Belle Époque glory. Most of the 71 rooms and 71 suites are decorated in soft pastel hues and include excellent woodwork, and most have a shaded private patio with views of the hotel's magnificent French-style gardens. The 15 prestige suites' names and furnishings pay homage to prominent guests who have been at the hotel in the past, including Marcel Proust, Coco Chanel, and  the Duke of Windsor. Privacy is guaranteed here, with a discreet underground tunnel providing unseen arrivals and departures from the hotel for guests who value the utmost in discretion.

Mandarin Oriental Paris

Mandarin Oriental is located in the heart of Paris, on rue Saint-Honoré, one of the world's most fashionable streets. The hotel emanates a timeless elegance with exquisite, contemporary décor, and it is surrounded by high couture and only steps from the Louvre. Beautifully designed and luxuriously appointed, the 138 rooms and 39 suites are among the most stylish and spacious in the city. The Mandarin Oriental's bar and restaurants are among the best in Paris, serving cutting-edge cuisine, delectable light dishes, and seductive cocktails in a sophisticated setting.

The Peninsula Paris

With the advent of the Peninsula Paris in August 2014, Hong Kong-style luxury arrived in the City of Light (albeit two years behind schedule). Some of France's greatest artisans were hand-picked to undertake the restoration of this late 19th century classic Haussmanian edifice and turn it into a luxury hotel, which took six years to complete. The hotel is located at 19 Avenue Kléber in the heart of Paris, only steps from the Arc de Triomphe and close to some of the world's most famous landmarks, museums, and luxury shopping districts. The 200 rooms and suites are designed for maximum comfort, ensuring a restful night's sleep. Crisp bed linens, marble bathrooms with customized mood lighting, and hallmark Peninsula technology, including complimentary high-speed wireless internet for all guests, give each room a sense of tranquility and modernity.

7 Affordable Hotels in Paris

Hotel De Seine

Hotel De Seine is at a fantastic location and offers great pricing. Located on the left side of the Seine, and so the name (rive gauche). It's on the edge of the Latin Quarter, which has a better restaurant scene than Le Marais, and is within walking distance to the Louvre, Notre Dame, Ile Saint Louis, and the Luxembourg Gardens.

This location and price are fantastic. They have a traditional design that makes you feel like an aristocrat while being affordable.

Hotel De Flore

The district of Montmartre is notable for three things. Burlesque shows at the Moulin Rouge and other "adult" venues are the first stop. Second, the Sacre-Coeur Basilica offers spectacular elevation views of Paris. Finally, there's a fantastic local culinary scene. This hotel is a clean and affordable option in a nice neighborhood with easy access to center Paris.

Hôtel Jeanne D'Arc Le Marais

Hôtel Jeanne d'Arc is a reasonably priced hotel with a wonderful location, clean and trendy. No, you won't be staying in the suite where Joséphine Bonaparte once stayed, but do you really need to? The Louvre and the Latin Quarter are nearby. Le Marais has a fantastic restaurant scene.

Les Jardins De Mademoiselle

Les Jardins de Mademoiselle is a hip hotel in Paris's 15th arrondissement, close to the Eiffel Tower and the Champ de Mars. Unlike the Ritz or the Four Seasons, this hotel is not too expensive.

Hotel Eiffel Blomet

This is a fantastic deal in terms of location, affordability, and value. The price is exceptionally inexpensive for a four-star hotel in the heart of Paris with such high ratings.

Hôtel Du Haut Marais

This hotel is a "go-to" hotel for business trips. It offers a lot of space in a modern, but cool room right in the center of Paris. Clean beds that are comfortable with all the amenities you'd want and sometimes even more. Some rooms have cool soaker tubs that work great for a romantic stay or after a long day of walking around Paris! The hotel claims "Le Marais" but is about a block outside the unofficial boundaries.

Hotel Monte Cristo

The Hotel Monte Cristo offers a wonderful middle-eastern ambiance that makes it enjoyable to stay at. Given its central position, central style and excellent evaluations, the price is actually rather reasonable. The hotel is in a good position; however, it is not within walking distance to the Seine. This location is on the outskirts of the Latin Quarter, which is packed with amazing pubs, restaurants and nightlife. It's also close to a few well-connected metro stations that can take you to the Eiffel Tower or other nearby attractions.

The Best Hotels in Paris for Each Category

Best for a Really Tight Budget: Generator Paris

Generator Paris is a hip designer hostel in the heart of Paris's vibrant 10th arrondissement. There is free Wi-Fi access, as well as a modern lounge space with a game room. At the on-site Café Fabien, you may eat regionally-inspired delicacies while listening to DJs and sipping a drink from the bar. Air-conditioning, bed linens, and a private bathroom with a shower are included in each of the modern rooms. A private terrace is included in some rooms.

Every morning, a continental breakfast is served at this hostel. A 24-hour front desk, a laundry room and a patio are also available as well as a communal lounge with a North African flair.

A five-minute walk to Canal Saint-Martin is lined with bars, restaurants and vintage shops. The hostel is half a kilometer from the Gare de l'Est Metro Station and a little less than a kilometer from Buttes-Chaumont Park.

Best for Escaping the City: Okko Hotels

The Okko Hotels Paris Porte De Versailles is located 701 meters from Paris Expo - Porte de Versailles Exhibition Center and 1.7 kilometers from Parc des Princes. It features air-conditioned rooms with free Wi-Fi access. The Eiffel Tower is located a little over two miles away from the hotel.

A flat-screen TV with satellite channels is provided in each room. In the rooms, there is a Nespresso machine as well as an iPod dock. They have their own bathroom. Free toiletries and a hairdryer are provided for your convenience. Every morning, a breakfast buffet is served. Soft drinks are also complimentary in the lounge during the day, and visitors can enjoy an appetizer buffet with antipasti, fresh vegetables, dips, and seasonal items in the evening.

Best for Stopovers: CitizenM

The CitizenM Paris Gare de Lyon is located in Paris's 12th district. It is close to the Gare de Lyon train station and has views of the Seine.

Large mattresses, a powerful rain shower, complimentary movies and iPads that control the entire room are all standard in each room. A mini fridge, hairdryers and custom-made toiletries are also included in the rooms. A tray is used to serve the continental breakfast.

CanteenM, a 24-hour desk and food and beverage area, serves draft beers, barista-made coffees, and some of the greatest cocktails in town. A rooftop bar with views of the city is also available.

Best for a Fun Weekend: Idol Hotel

The Idol Hotel is a 15-minute walk from Galeries Lafayette and 100 meters from Saint-Lazare Train Station in Paris. The hotel was designed to reflect the groovy and funky music of the 1960s and 1980s.

The Idol Hotel rooms include a telephone and a flat-screen TV with satellite channels. The bathroom includes complimentary toiletries and a hair dryer. Every day, a continental breakfast is served. A minibar and a coffee machine are also available in each room.

Pigalle is 0.8 miles from the hotel, while the Opéra Garnier is 0.7 miles away. A 20-minute stroll will take you to the Champs-Elysées.

Best for Location: Hotel Jeanne d'Arc

The Hôtel Jeanne d'Arc Le Marais is located in Paris' Marais area, just a 2-minute walk from the Place des Vosges Square. A desk, wardrobe, and flat-screen TV with satellite channels are included in every room. Free toiletries and a bath or shower are provided in the private bathroom.

Each morning, Hôtel Jeanne d'Arc Le Marais serves a continental breakfast with French pastries, butter, and jam. The property is within walking distance of several restaurants.

The Louver Museum is a three-minute walk from the Saint-Paul Metro Station, which provides direct access. The hotel is seven minutes' walk from the Place de la Bastille. There is free Wi-Fi provided throughout the hotel.

Best for Families: Camping de Paris

The Place des Vosges Square is merely a two-minute walk from Hôtel Jeanne d'Arc Le Marais, which is located in Paris' Marais area.

Best for Peace and Quiet: Hotel Passy Eiffel

The Eiffel Tower is only 701 meters away from Passy Eiffel, which offers the best views of the Eiffel Tower. It provides 3-star rooms on a quiet and secure street in Paris. The rooms at Passy Eiffel are modern in design and include a minibar and a television with satellite channels. All of the rooms are air-conditioned, and some of them feature views of the Eiffel Tower. A continental breakfast is available in the breakfast room or in the guest rooms. The Arc de Triomphe, Champs Elysées and Montparnasse are all within walking distance.

Best for a Friendly Welcome: Hotel Port Royal

Conveniently set in the 5th arr. District of Paris, Port Royal Hotel is located a 20-minute walk from Luxembourg Gardens, 2.6 km from Sainte Chapelle and 2.6 km from Notre Dame.

Among the facilities at this property are a 24-hour front desk and a shared lounge. The property is 3.9 km from Louvre Museum and within 3.4 km of the city center. A continental breakfast is available daily at the accommodation.

Best for Chic Simplicity: Oh la la! Hotel

Ideally situated in the 11th arr. Oh, Parisian district, Oh la la! The Sainte-Chapelle is 3 kilometers away, the Louvre Museum is 3.1 kilometers away, and Notre Dame Cathedral is 3.1 kilometers away. The 3-star hotel has air-conditioned rooms with free WiFi and a bar. The property is allergy-free and is at a short distance from the Opéra Bastille.

Best for Hanging Out: Hoxton Paris

The Hoxton, Paris is located in the heart of Paris, just 230 meters from the Grands Boulevards Metro Station. The on-site restaurant is available to guests. After a long day, some rooms provide a seating space where you may unwind. The Hoxton, Paris offers complimentary Wi-Fi access throughout the property. There is a television.

The Hoxton, Paris is 1.5 kilometers from the Louvre Museum and the Pompidou Centre. The Hoxton, Paris is 18 kilometers from the nearest airport, Paris - Orly Airport.

Best for Kooky Interiors: Mama Shelter Paris West

Mama Shelter Paris West is offering accommodation in Paris. The property is set 700 m from Paris Expo - Porte de Versailles, 5 km from Rodin Museum and 5 km from Parc des Princes. Eiffel Tower is 5 km from the hotel and Luxembourg Gardens is 5 km away. At the hotel, all rooms come with air conditioning, free Wi-Fi and free movies on-demand. They feature a private bathroom with a hairdryer and toiletries. A buffet breakfast is served each morning at the property. The accommodation offers a terrace.

Best for Flea Market Fans: Mob Hotel

MOB HOTEL Paris Les Puces offers pet-friendly accommodation in Saint-Ouen, 500 m from Garibaldi Metro Station and 800 m from Mairie Saint-Ouen Metro Station. Free Wi-Fi is available throughout the hotel and guests can enjoy the on-site restaurant and bar. Guests can also enjoy a garden.

Certain rooms have a seating area where you can relax. A terrace or balcony are featured in certain rooms. The air-conditioned rooms are equipped with a private bathroom. For your comfort, you will find free organic toiletries and a hairdryer. Other amenities such as a giant table football and pop-up stores are available at the hotel.

Bar des 2 Moulins (Rue Lepic) is 2.3 km from MOB HOTEL Paris Les Puces, while La Cité du Cinéma is 1.8 km away. Paris - Charles de Gaulle Airport is 20 km from the property.

Best Time to Visit Paris

The best season to visit Paris is between April and June, and October and early November, when the weather is temperate and pleasant, and tourist throngs are lower than during the summer. Early December, January, and February are the cheapest months to visit Paris. June is the ideal month to visit Paris.

Best Time to Book Hotels

The Best Paris Hotels and Best Paris Hotels for Families are sometimes sold-out months in advance. Book at least four months in advance of your trip.

Best Time for Shopping

In France, sales are regulated by the government, and retail discounts are only permitted twice a year, during two six-week periods known as Les Soldes (The Sales). The winter sales run from early January to mid-February, while the summer sales run from late June to mid-July. Because discounts are uncommon and limited, expect the top Parisian boutiques to be packed and chaotic during these times, particularly on Fridays and Saturdays. Sundays are mostly off limits for shopping. As the weeks pass, the crowds thin out, but the stock of reduced items grows. Specific sales dates vary from year to year; a fast internet search can tell you when to go if you want to be first in line, or when to avoid if you want a more relaxed shopping experience.

Best Time to Avoid Crowds

Paris had around 30 million visitors every year. From May to September, there will be crowds, but July will be the busiest (followed closely by June and August). If avoiding crowds is your primary goal, we recommend going between October and April. The months of October and April are the greatest for mild weather and avoiding crowds. While going during the holidays in December is also a lovely time to go, the number of tourists tends to increase from mid-December until the end of the year.

Average Weather in Paris by Month

As travelers, we've discovered the weather isn't always as dependable as we believe. Though Paris has cold spells and heat waves, these are the average temps throughout the year. The rainiest month is December and the driest month is June.

January: 39.7 F - 44.4 F
February: 40.4 F - 46.6 F
March: 45.2 F - 52.9 F
April: 51.2 F - 59.4 F
May: 57.7 F - 65.5 F
June: 63.9 F - 71.8 F
July: 67.6 F -75.6 F
August: 66.9 F - 75.3 F
September: 61.5 F - 69.6 F
October: 54.7 F - 61.5 F
November: 46.2 F - 51.3 F
December: 40.7 F - 45.4 F

Best Time for Museums

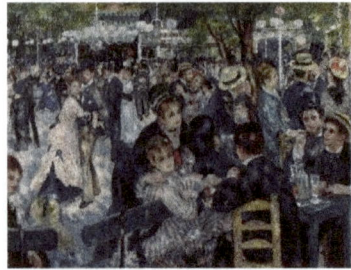

The midwinter tourism slump means shorter lines and less crowds, making January and February ideal months for visiting Paris museums and galleries. A Paris Museum Pass, which offers unlimited entrance to over 50 museums and monuments in and around the city, may be purchased at any time of year and allows travelers to skip the lines entirely. Consider visiting at night to avoid crowds — most museums and galleries are open at least once a week in the evening hours, and crowds thin out after nightfall. In addition, several museums in Paris provide free admission on the first Sunday of each month, which is a terrific deal for anyone looking to see art and antiquities on the cheap, but be aware that the first Sunday of each month is also the first Sunday of the month. Furthermore, many museums in Paris provide free entrance on the first Sunday of each month, which is a terrific deal for anyone looking to see art and antiquities on the cheap, but keep in mind that galleries may be very packed on these days.

Best Time for Flowers and Gardens

Though each year is different, the earliest blossoms in Paris' gardens and parks normally appear in mid- to late April, when spring bulbs and trees begin to bloom. Summer perennial beds are re-planted in late May and early June, so there's a slight delay in flowers, but they're usually well established by July. The famed rose gardens at Parc de Bagatelle and L'Ha-les-Roses bloom in late May and early June as well. Gardens throughout the city will be in bloom throughout the summer and into the early fall. September is a particularly lovely month to explore Parisian gardens, as the blooms are still plentiful but the crowds have lessened.

Best Time for Holiday Displays

The City of Lights celebrates Christmas early, with beautiful seasonal lights adorning the city during the last two months of the year. Early to mid-November sees Parisian department stores unveil their magnificent displays and set up Christmas trees, and by the end of the month, the Champ Elysees is decked out for the holidays. By the beginning of December, most additional seasonal light displays are up, and the marches de noel (Christmas markets) are open for business. Christmas decorations and marketplaces are up and going far into January.

Best Time to Visit Disneyland Paris

Disneyland is usually busiest while school is not in session, which includes not just the summer months and around Christmas, but also weekends and the end of October, when many European schools are on leave. Midweek (Tuesday through Thursday) from mid-January to mid-March and mid-April to mid-May are the best times for shorter lines and less crowds. In the winter, lines are shorter, but you'll encounter cooler temperatures and certain rides closed for renovations — generally no more than two or three at a time.

Some Best Things To do

Best Advice: Take a tour! The tours and guides in Paris are fantastic.

Get Your Guide: A fantastic resource for finding excursions and getting great deals.

Skip The Line Tickets: Eiffel Tower • Louvre • Versailles • Disneyland Paris • Arc de Triomphe • Catacombs • Musee d'Orsay

Chocolate Tasting Tour: A three-hour walking tour of Saint-Germain-des-Prés featuring five chocolate tastes, three pastries, and a variety of breads. Strongly suggested.

Behind The Scenes Bakery Tour: Baguettes are made in a traditional French bakery. Lots much enjoyment. Also, worth checking out: Macaron Cooking Class.

Fat Tire Bike Tours: These are a lot of fun. There are bikes for people of various ages and sizes. The Paris Tour (3.5 hours) • Versailles Tour (3.5 hours) are all recommended tours (8 hours)

Eiffel Tower & Seine River Cruise: Skip the line at the Eiffel Tower then take a 1-hour cruise along the River Seine.

4 Days in Paris
Travel
Itinerary

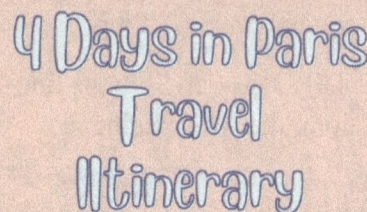

Day 1

The Left Bank,
Saint-Germain,
and the Eiffel Tower

Day 2

Gothic Churches, A Food
Tour, and the Louvre

Day 3

The Coolest Neighborhoods
in Paris (Montmartre, le
Marais, Canal St. Martin,
and Montorgueil)

Day 4

A Day Trip to
Versailles

4-Day Travel Itinerary

Day 1: The Left Bank, Saint-Germain, and the Eiffel Tower

Start your first day with a walking tour to establish your bearings and learn some local tips and recommendations, then head to the Left Bank for sunset and an evening at the Eiffel Tower.

1. It normally includes several of the city's major sights (though Paris is large enough that you won't be able to see them all in a couple of hours) as well as historical and cultural context. You probably won't go into the Louvre, but you'll pass by and briefly discuss it. This will give you a good overview and allow you to pick what you want to revisit later.

2. You'll learn about the city from a local's perspective, including what to eat and drink, how to get around, the best way to see the Louvre, and other extremely helpful insider information. Additionally, you'll gain crucial insight into Parisian society that you can only obtain by speaking with a local.

3. If you're lucky, your tour guide will send you a list of restaurants, bars, things to do and see, and more at the end of

your tour, which you can use to explore the city on your own later. We love getting our hands on those lists, and have used them extensively on our travels to discover places we definitely wouldn't have found on our own.

After your tour, grab a bite to eat in Saint-Germain (we recommend LouLou for brunch or Georgette for French food), then make your way to the Eiffel Tower through the bougie paradise that is Saint-Germain.

This is a rough map of our path through Saint-Germain. Along the road, there are several places to dine and drink, including Ladurée for macarons, Grom for gelato, and La Quincave for wine.

Head to the 6th Arrondissement, directly across the street from the Le Bon Marché department store, a 19th-century French institution that sells upscale apparel, beauty products, and gourmet foods.

We adore Les Grand Epiceries de Paris, a posh grocery shop with a vast assortment of artisanal breads, pastries, cheeses, and other specialty foods all under one roof.

Grab a coffee at Ten Belles on Rue du Cherche-Midi before heading to the Jardin du Luxembourg, where you can relax amid the flowers and soak up the sun.

You'll pass the present Senate meeting venue, the Palais du Luxembourg, on your way up to Rue Bonaparte. Arrive to the Église Saint-Sulpice, which is well known as the scene for The Da Vinci Code. The church took 150 years to construct and contains some stunning frescoes by Delacroix.

Return to Rue Bonaparte to see Saint-Germain-des-Près, the oldest standing church in Paris, established in the 11th century. The famous Café de Flore and Les Deux Magots, where artists, writers, and socialites spent all of their time at the turn of the twentieth century, may be seen from here. Sip coffee outside or peer inside to see the

stunning interiors, which have remained largely untouched for almost a century.

Continue your stroll down the Boulevard Saint-Germain, stopping at La Dernière Goutte for an optional diversion to browse an exceptional selection of wines and pick up a bottle for your evening picnic. The Fromagerie Laurent Dubois will satisfy any cheese lover, and your self-guided walking tour will conclude at the lovely Shakespeare & Company, an iconic new and used bookstore  that has been drawing book enthusiasts since 1951.

Walk west down the Seine to your next destination of the day, the world's best collection of Impressionist art.

The Eiffel Tower, one of the most iconic images you'll see during your four days in Paris, can be seen from all over central Paris, including stunning views from the Seine's bridges (the Pont d'Iéna connects the Jardins du Trocadéro with the Champ de Mars, where the tower stands) and the Hôtel des Invalides (which is worth checking out during your walks around the city for its golden roofs and imposing stature).

We recommend traveling to the top of the Arc de Triomphe or the Tour Montparnasse if you want a postcard-perfect perspective of

Paris, as the Eiffel Tower will be included in the view. The trouble with seeing the Eiffel Tower from the top is that you can't see the Eiffel Tower.

The allure of climbing it, on the other hand, is undeniable. To get to the top, you can either use the elevators to the second or third floor viewing decks, or walk up to the second-floor platform, which requires about 1,500 stairs in total.

Day 2: Gothic Churches, A Food Tour, and the Louvre

Start your second day in Paris by seeing two of the world's most impressive Gothic churches before plunging into Paris' food culture with a cooking/baking lesson or a food tour to sample some of the city's best dishes as recommended by residents.

After that, spend the afternoon and early evening in the Louvre, where you may explore one of the world's largest art collections. Ideally, with a tour guide.

Start your day early if you want to see two of Paris' outstanding examples of Gothic architecture. Both are churches, by the way.

The Notre Dame Cathedral is a must-see for medieval art lovers and those wishing to meander through some of the loveliest church aisles. You may stroll through quite fast, enjoying the gothic arches and beautiful stained-glass windows, depending on how much detail you

want to take in. Climb to the top of the tower for spectacular views.

If you're in Paris on a nice day and want to spend a couple of hours admiring some of the world's best stained-glass windows, we highly recommend Sainte-Chappelle.

This tiny gem of a church is just a few blocks away from the Palais de Justice. The church is a tiny, perhaps not particularly intimidating structure from the exterior, but the main show is inside. It is regarded as Paris' most beautiful Gothic landmark and is definitely worth a visit.

The best and most eclectic art collection of your vacation can be found at the Louvre. Even if you only plan on seeing a few attractions, the museum is worth spending at least three hours there. In the early 13th century, the massive palace served as a stronghold before becoming a national museum in 1793.

Later French governments, often controversially, added to the collection by bringing in art from all around Europe, as well as Assyrian, Etruscan, Greek, Coptic, and Islamic art and antiquities.

The Seine divides Paris into two parts: the Rive Gauche (Left Bank) and

the Rive Droite (Right Bank). If you have any energy left after your visit to the Louvre, we recommend strolling from there to the Arc de Triomphe.

The Jardin du Palais Royal - A lovely park in

the center of the city created around the Royal Palace in the 17th century. A wonderful spot to take a break and smell the roses.

Take a stroll through the Tuileries Gardens, where Parisians relax in the lounge chairs by the fountains or go for a walk with their friends. Cross it from the Louvre to the Place de la Concorde, and you'll find yourself at the large plaza with the Obelisk (it is 3,300 years old and engraved with Egyptian hieroglyphics).

Continue along the Seine to the Grand Palais, which was created for the 1900 World's Fair and now houses many exhibitions. Take a look at the incredible 8.5-ton art nouveau glass roof!

Finish your trek by wandering down the Champs-Élysées towards the Arc de Triomphe.

Day 3: Explore the Coolest Neighborhoods in Paris

There are no tourist attractions on the agenda today (in the classic sense). Instead, we propose taking a long self-guided walk around the Rive Droite and some of Paris' most intriguing neighborhoods from west to east (approximately).

Montmartre, the jewel atop the hill where you'll find Sacré-Coeur and picturesque cobblestone lanes, Le Marais, Canal St. Martin and Montorgueil are among those neighborhoods. Following our recent vacation to Paris, the latter two have become our new favorite spots.

Montmartre is recommended as an afternoon/evening trip by several guides, both books and travel blogs. It's easy to see why: the sunset view is breathtaking (you're looking into the sun from Sacré-Coeur at sunrise), the romantic emotions linger after dark, and the area comes alive with people.

We preferred Montmartre first thing in the morning, before the crowds arrived. That is why we have you here at the start of the day rather than towards the end.

Start your day at KB Coffee Roasters, which has two advantages. One, their patio at the base of Montmartre is an exceptionally delightful location to have your morning coffee in the Parisian sun, replete with a carousel, which in my opinion is a very Parisian occurrence. Second, their coffee is excellent.

Make your way up the slope to the peak of Montmartre from there. You have the option of taking the steep stairs straight up the hill or meandering up the twisting cobblestone streets. The white church on the

hill, Sacré-Coeur, is at the top of the hill and has one of my favorite vistas in Paris.

Finish with a stroll down Rue des Abbesses, Montmartre's buzzing center of action. It is surrounded with stores and restaurants and is well worth a stroll.

Le Marais, which literally means "marsh," was converted to farmland in the 12th century and became a popular district when Henry IV erected the Place Royale in the early 17th century (now the Place des Vosges).

It is now home to many designer boutiques as well as unique pubs and eateries.

The trendiest neighborhood is slowly migrating north, with Haut Marais (upper Marais) increasingly attracting rising stars with vintage fashion and sophisticated restaurants.

Canal St. Martin is one of our new favorite Paris areas, partly because it feels like a real Parisian neighborhood. There are young families and young couples walking along the canal.

It's a short walk from the 4th Arrondissement to the canal in the 10th Arrondissement, which is northeast of where your Le Marais trip ends.

Take a large loop around the canal, stop for food, drinks and whatever else your heart desires along the route.

La Cidrerie was one of our favorite places. We love cider, and La Cidrerie is the place to go to sample many types of French cider. We arrived at opening time and chatted with the proprietor while he poured us a variety of French Ciders. They also had one of our favorite American ciders, Stem Ciders' Chile Guava, on tap, which was a pleasant surprise! We highly recommend it if you want to sample French cider as well as a variety of other ciders from across the world.

The 2nd Arrondissement's Rue Montorgueil spans north to south and is one of the best areas in the city for supper and drinks (in our opinion, anyway). We stayed close (in Sentier, a 2nd Arrondissement sub-neighborhood) and fell in love with the region.

Within a few blocks, there's so much to eat and drink! There seems to be a classic Parisian restaurant on every corner, complete with outdoor seating and people smoking while eating and drinking.

Day 4: A Day Trip to Versailles

A visit to the Sun King's palace will literally round off your four-day journey to Paris. In the 17th century, Louis XIV transformed his father's hunting lodge on the outskirts of Paris into the gigantic Château de Versailles, making it France's most famous and finest site.

It's huge and beautiful at the same time, with all the extravagant decorations you'd expect. Make time for the immaculately kept gardens studded with sculptures, as well as several noteworthy stops.

The best method to travel to Versailles is to take the RER C from central Paris (be sure you get out at the Versailles Château stop, not the Porte de Versailles, which is on the 12 line).

Trains run every 15 minutes starting at 5:30 a.m., so arrive early (the trip takes around 40 minutes from Invalides, to give you an idea). Tickets cost €3.65 and can be purchased at the station from which you are departing. As you depart the station, there will be helpful signage.

To get the most out of your vacation to Versailles, it is recommended to spend a whole day there. When you purchase your tickets online, you will be given a time slot for your visit, which will assist you in planning your day.

Instead of carrying an audio guide, you can download a free mobile app. It also includes maps and further information.

A complete ticket costs €20 and gives you entrance to the entire estate, which allows you to see the palace, gardens and whatever else you have time for.

Because the Château and grounds are so large, hiring a tour is the best way to see everything. However, there are a few activities that must be completed:

The Royal Apartments are worth seeing.

Imagine yourself at a ball as you go through the Hall of Mirrors.

Take a stroll through the gardens and pay a visit to the Bassin de Neptune, which features 99 fountains.

If possible, plan your visit around the Musical Fountains Shows (daily and nightly exhibitions of water "dancing" to music that take place during the summer).

Cost to Travel to Paris

What amount of cash will you require for your vacation to Paris?

On average, travelers to Paris spend roughly €184 ($200) each day, which is the average daily price based on other visitors' spending. Previous tourists have spent an average of €31 ($34) on meals and €17 ($18) on local transportation in a single day.

In addition, a couple's hotel in Paris costs $263 on average. So, a one-week trip to Paris for two costs $2,797 on the average. These average travel rates were compiled from previous travelers to assist you in planning your own trip budget.

A one-week holiday in Paris costs approximately €1,286 for one person. So, a one-week trip to Paris for two people costs roughly €2,572. In Paris, a two-week holiday for two people costs €5,144. When traveling as a family of three or four, the cost per person frequently decreases because children's tickets are less expensive and hotel rooms can be shared. Your daily budget will decrease if you go slower for a longer period of time. A monthly budget for two individuals traveling together in Paris is generally less than a weekly budget for one person traveling alone.

Accommodation Budget in Paris

The average cost of a single night's stay in Paris is €121. The average hotel stay in Paris costs €242 for two persons sharing a standard double-occupancy room.

Transportation Budget in Paris

In Paris, a taxi ride is substantially more expensive than public transit. Past visitors to Paris have paid an average of €17 per person, per day on local transportation.

Food Budget in Paris

While meal costs in Paris vary, the average daily food expense in Paris is €31. Based on past tourists' spending tendencies, an average lunch in Paris should cost roughly €12 per person while dining out. Breakfast is frequently less expensive than lunch or dinner.

Entertainment Budget in Paris

In Paris, entertainment and leisure cost on average €62 per person each day. This covers prices for museum and attraction admission tickets, day tours, and other sightseeing charges.

Tips and Handouts Budget in Paris

In Paris, the average daily tip and handout cost is €19. In Paris, a tip is usually between 5% and 15% of the bill.

Scams, Robberies, and Mishaps Budget in Paris

On a trip, awful things can sometimes happen. You'll just have to deal with it! In Paris, the average cost of a scam, robbery, or mishap is €148.

Alcohol Budget in Paris

In Paris, the average person spends roughly €19 per day on alcoholic beverages. Despite your bigger budget, the more you spend on booze, the more fun you may have.

Water Budget

In Paris, people spend €1.99 per day on bottled water on average. The water at Paris's public fountains is considered safe to drink.

References

Photo Credit

Stasknop – stock.adobe.com - Centre Georges Pompidou glows in the night, Paris, France, pg. 10.

Mistervlad – stock.adobe.com – Paris, France – May 2019; Louvre palace and pyramid at night, pg. 12.

Elna Dijour – stock.adobe.com – Paris, France – January 28, 2017: Chanel shop in old Marais quarter. Chanel fashion house founded by Coco Chanel is symbol of haute couture and luxury goods. Sepia historic photo, pg. 14.

Kovalenkovpetre – stock.adobe.com – The legendary Hotel de Crillon is the luxury 5-star hotel in Paris. It overlooks the famed Place del la Concord. It ranked among the most luxurious hotels in the world, pg. 15.

EdNurg – stock.adobe.com – 26 July 2019, Paris, France: Modern art Sculptures in the Stravinsky fountain near Centre Popidou, pg. 18.

Patryk Kosmider – stock.adobe.com – Paris, France – September 18, 2022: Architecture of Grand Palais des Champs-Elysees in Paris, France, pg. 19.

Kruwt – stock.adobe.com – People shopping in luxury Lafayette department store of Paris, France, pg. 20.

Dinadesign – stock.adobe.com – View of the Moulin Rouge (Red Mill) at night in Paris, France, pg. 25.

Fl1photo – stock.adobe.com – The Moulin Rouge in Paris, France, pg. 32.

Dbrnjhrj – stock.adobe.com – Night performance near Sleeping Beauty castle in Disneyland Paris. Disneyland Paris (Euro Disney Resort) – entertainment resort in Marne-la-Vallee. Marne-la-Vallee, France. March 30, 2019, pg. 37.

Kovalenkovpetre – stock.adobe.com – Paris, France-November 30, 2019: The cabaret Crazy Horse is the most iconic of all the Parisian cabarets located at avenue George V in Paris, France, pg. 38.

Nadirco – stock.adobe.com – Paris Louvre Museum by Night, pg. 41.

Agcreativelab – stock.adobe.com – Paris, France – May 6, 2017: Mona Lisa at the Louvre Museum. Paris, France, pg. 41.

GiorgioMorara – stock.adobe.com – Claude Monet (1840-1296) Impression, Sunrise, 1872, oil on canvas. Marmottan Monet Museum, Paris, pg. 44.

OliverFoerstner – stock.adobe.com - Paris, France – May 12, 2017: Architectural details on the façade of the Centre Pompidou. The Centre Pompidou is home to the National Museum of Modern Art, pg. 44.

Bruno Bleu – stock.adobe.com – Porte d'entrée du 59 Rivoli. After Squat. Le 59 Rivoli, anciennement Chez Robert: electrons libres, collectif d'artistes base au numero 59 de la rue do Rivoli, Paris. France. 28/09/21, pg. 46

Florence Piot – stock.adobe.com – Façade et enseigne de l'hotel de luxe "Hotel de Crillon, a Rosewood hotel" a Paris, celebre palace parisien sur la place de la Concorde – novembre 2020, pg. 54.

Bruno – stock.adobe.com – Paris, France. July 14. 2022. Façade of the five-star luxury Peninsula hotel, pg. 56.

MarinadeArt – stock.adobe.com – Paris, France – December 11, 2016: Typical French street in Montmartre district with small houses are located cafes, restaurants and art galleries, pg. 56.

Hippomyta – stock.adobe.com – Sleeping Beauty castle in Fantasyland at Disneyland Paris in Paris, France on March 5, 2013, pg. 77.

UlyssePixel – stock.adobe.com – Paris, France – March 15 2020: Café de Flore, pg. 83.

Zefart – stock.adobe.com – Paris, France – May 08, 2017: Shakespeare and Company bookstore and Library on the Seine riverbank in Paris, first opened by Sylvia Beach on 19 November 1919, pg. 84.

EwaStudio – stock.adobe.com – Paris, France – February 15, 2018: Interior of the Louvre, the world's largest art museum and a historic monument in Paris, France, pg. 87.

David Henry – stock.adobe.com – A sunset over rue des Abbesses, pg. 90.

Takashi Images – stock.adobe.com – Versailles, France – May 25 2016: The chapel of the Royal Palace of Versailles in France. The Royal Palace of Versailles is on the UNESCO World Heritage List, pg. 93.

Anecaroline – stock.adobe.com – Chambre de Madame Victoire au rez-de-chaussee du chateau de Versailles, Yvelines, pg. 94.

Takashi Images – stock.adobe.com – Versailles, France – May 25 2016: The Hall of Mirrors (Galerie de Glaces) of the Royal Palace of Versailles in France. The Royal Palace of Versailles is on the UNESCO World Heritage List, pg. 95.

EwaStudio – stock.adobe.com – Versailles, France – February 14, 2018: Interior of Chateau de Versailles, Versailles palace is in UNESCO World Heritage Site list since 1979, pg. 95.

Dbrnjhrj – stock.adobe.com – Palais-Royal (1639) – it was personal residence of Cardinal Richelieu in Paris. Columns Buren (The Colonness de Buren, 1985) – 260 black and white striped columns. Paris, France. May 13, 2014, pg. 98.

References

https://en.wikipedia.org/wiki/Paris

https://linkparis.com/the-history-of-paris-france/

https://www.meininger-hotels.com/blog/en/fun-facts-paris/

https://takelessons.com/live/french/useful-french-phrases-travelers-z04

https://insidr.co/french-etiquette-and-manners-to-know-before-coming-to-paris/

https://www.thrillist.com/travel/nation/french-etiquette-tips

https://www.pexels.com/photo/picture-of-eiffel-tower-338515/

https://tourscanner.com/blog/paris-bucket-list-top-places-to-visit/

https://unsplash.com/photos/9s5MWNVwDXQ

https://devourtours.com/blog/best-restaurants-paris/

https://theluxurytravelexpert.com/2021/08/02/top-10-best-luxury-hotels-paris/

https://thetourguy.com/travel-blog/france/paris/hotels-paris/best-most-affordable-paris-hotels-this-year/

https://www.independent.co.uk/travel/hotels/paris-best-budget-hotels-cheap-families-boutique-latin-quarter-france-generator-b1965896.html

https://santorinidave.com/best-time-to-visit-paris

https://www.travelandleisure.com/travel-tips/best-time-to-visit-paris

https://worldinparis.com/4-days-in-paris-itinerary

https://www.budgetyourtrip.com/france/paris

https://www.timeout.com/paris/en/attractions/best-paris-attractions

https://www.france-hotel-guide.com/en/blog/quirky-places/

https://wheatlesswanderlust.com/4-days-in-paris-itinerary/

www.ingramcontent.com/pod-product-compliance
Lightning Source LLC
Chambersburg PA
CBHW071208120626
46546CB00006B/2463